ENLIGHTENMENT

by David Bognar

D1451261

NEW WAY
MANCHESTER, CONNECTICUT

Enlightenment
by David Bognar

Published by
New Way
540 Vernon St.
Manchester, CT 06042

© 2010 by New Way

Cover Design – Linda Tajirian
Book Design – David Bognar
Pat Minicucci
Photography – David Bognar
Photo Editing – Pat Minicucci

Printed in the United States of America
Photo Edition, First Printing: April 2010
ISBN 13: 978-1-929860-06-7
ISBN 10: 1-929860-06-4
Library of Congress Control Number: 2010920002

www.EnlightenmentMadeSimple.com

Contents

Contents

Introduction

I ALWAYS WANTED TO know the answers to the big questions of life. Who am I? What's it all about? Why are we here? Is there a god? Life after death? What is the meaning of life? Is goat cheese really better for me?

Most people think there's no way to know the answers to these questions because they think they are matters of belief or faith. Wrong. It's like someone saying there's no way of knowing how toasters work. Sure, if you were unaware of, and never took the time to study the body of knowledge that exists about toasters, you might believe their inner workings are unknowable. Not true.

This book is the culmination of more than forty years of research. I conducted a logical, honest, and what I would characterize as a scientific inquiry into what the hell is going on. I wasn't invested in any outcome. I just wanted to know. I was willing to accept that there was no god, and atheism suited me quite well for many years. But I eventually encountered information that made it undeniably evident that something was happening that could not be explained by conventional science.

Remarkably, there is a huge body of evidence. If people had the time to study the same materials I did, I am confident they would come to a similar conclusion—there's far more to reality than we think. Wiser people before me have discovered these truths. Greek philosophers called it "theosophia" or "divine wisdom." It has been referred to as "the perennial philosophy," "the great tradition" and "the wisdom of the ages." For thousands of years, this knowledge has been passed on through various spiritual disciplines, secret religious societies, and esoteric writings. Some have discovered it through scientific inquiry into natural and metaphysical phenomena. Others have found this knowledge through revelatory experience or "gnosis," which means directly experienced spiritual knowledge. In recent years, the study of psychology and physics have provided us with greater understanding, and proof, as science comes full circle with the "esoteric science," of this wisdom of the ages. That's where the good news begins.

At the root of this wisdom is the essential experience commonly referred to as "enlightenment." Amazing as it might seem, enlightenment is actually simple.

It just Is.

Wait, "If it just 'Is', how come I'm not experiencing it?" Well, it does take some doing (actually it takes some "being", which involves making an effort to remember to *choose*. Some have described this as an "effortless effort"...but I'm getting ahead of myself.)

For me, it's all about providing information that can help people. The divine wisdom joined with the psychology of spiritual growth has the potential to significantly help people cope with fear and obtain what they desire in life. Access to this knowledge should not be limited only to spiritual masters and those with sufficient time to read and study such a large volume of information. Until now, no one has gathered all of this information and presented it in a concise, easy-to-read format. This book is intended to provide a quick, contemporary synthesis of the basics of this ageless wisdom and its psycho-spiritual fundamentals, with the goal of helping to alleviate some of the suffering that is so prevalent on this planet.

Big Questions...

The truth will set you free,
but first…
it will scare the hell out of you.

Big Questions

LIFE IS FUNNY. Quirky funny. All this talk about reality being an illusion never made sense to me, until lately.

There's a Buddhist version of the story of Adam and Eve about a man in an empty room—empty, except for an incredibly beautiful piece of sculpture. He spends all his free time in the room because the sculpture gives him profound pleasure and joy. One day, he thinks maybe if he had another sculpture he'd be even happier. So he buys another beautiful piece of sculpture and puts it in the room and it does make him happier...for awhile. So, he gets another one, thinking it will make him at least as happy as he was before. That worked too—for awhile. To make a long parable short, the room eventually became so crowded with exquisite and beautiful art that the man couldn't experience the beauty of any one piece due to the distraction and clutter of the others. Eventually, he throws out all but the original and lives happily ever after.

This is a story about the universe and the creation of physical reality. Supposedly, once upon a time, before time, we were all one blissed-out energy field when some wise guy got the idea that maybe there's something better and bingo: poverty, pollution, and politicians. It's kind of like the human race got caught up in a bad dream and forgot it was dreaming. We keep coming back, lifetime after lifetime, trying to figure it out. We seem to know there's something or someplace else and some of us are trying to get back there, or here, or wherever it is.

When I was a kid, everything was love. I mean everything. It was as if there was no boundary between the love in me and around me. Life was a wonderful flow of love, curiosity, playing, and learning. Then something happened. I'm not sure what, but that experience of profound love faded with time and eventually disappeared.

I wanted that experience of love again. It seemed natural, the way it was supposed to be. Somehow it was clear to me that the love I had felt was always there even if I couldn't feel it. I couldn't explain it, but I knew that the experience was somewhere inside me and available to all of us. Somehow I knew, without a doubt, that love was the only thing that really mattered. I decided I was going to have that love in my life. I decided I would find out how, and when I did, I would share it with everyone who was willing to listen.

I studied psychology mostly. I started noticing remarkable correlations between science, eastern religions, physics, and para-psychology. After decades of reading, studying, workshops, seminars, psychics, mediums, egomaniacs, quacks, worse than quacks, (quacks with followings), diets, vitamins, pyramids, ghosts, garlic, juices, ginseng, ions, isolation tanks, running, jumping, hanging upside down, breathing in strange and unusual ways, innumerable meditations, psychotherapies and spiritual schools, I finally reached my goal. I understood what the hell was going on. The basics anyway. No big deal really. Turns out wiser guys then me had figured it out long ago. Anyone can if they want to. All the information is there. It may not all be in one place, but it's there.

Crazy? Maybe, but I don't think so. In fact, I think I'm going sane.

I want to share with you the essence of what I've learned. It's pretty simple really. The truth usually is. The problem is that a lot of people have a hard time accepting the truth. Our brains like to complicate things, and sometimes things are not as they appear to be. That's why most spiritual masters seldom come right out and tell you the plain truth. No one would believe them. We'd laugh in their faces. "What do you mean physical reality is an illusion? I asked you about the nature of reality and you tell me it's a holographic dream? Are you trying to be funny?"

It's not hard to imagine why gurus became cryptic with their, "You figure it out" kind of answers.

The concept of a god as a souped-up Santa with a white beard who knows when you've been bad and good never made sense to me. Logic, plus my unpleasant Catholic associations with God as a cosmic thought policeman ready to pulverize me for every adolescent male fantasy, created a negative knee-jerk reaction to the word "god." The idea of hell—a place where you fry like bacon for eternity for a few measly sins (some of which were about as natural as breathing) didn't appeal to me either. It didn't fit the idea of an all-loving all-forgiving, omnipotent type guy.

Having decided God did not exist, I was determined to find out what did, if anything. Evolving from fish and monkeys seemed plausible. But what of all these inexplicable phenomenon: the Bermuda triangle, ESP, PSI, pyramids, precognitive dreams, astral projection, near death experiences, Edgar Cayce, and tofu hotdogs? What had caused those? Some seemed to have reasonable explanations while others did not. I hadn't believed all of what I had read but some evidence was hard to deny. There were too many inexplicable events reported by rational people, including reputable scientists and researchers. There was so much evidence that a rational person couldn't deny that something extraordinary was going on, something that traditional science could not explain.

Like I said, life is funny.

The Unified Field

"A human being is a part of the whole called by us universe, a part limited in time and space. He experiences himself, his thoughts and feeling as something separated from the rest, a kind of optical delusion of his consciousness. This delusion is a kind of prison for us, restricting us to our personal desires and to affection for a few persons nearest to us. Our task must be to free ourselves from this prison by widening our circle of compassion to enhance all living creatures and the whole of nature in its beauty."

—Albert Einstein

The Unified Field

THE EXPLANATION BEGINS with the funny little thing called "the unified field."

Albert Einstein, eastern religions, spiritualists, and physicists agree that there is a unified field of energy that makes up our universe. Everything that exists is a different aspect of and integral part of this one unified field.

What is it exactly? According to many of these sources, it is a multifaceted, indescribably powerful, positively oriented energy gestalt. In other words, it's an intelligent, apparently benevolent energy. The fantastic organization and balance in nature and in the universe seem to support this theory. If there is only one energy that makes up everything, and that energy isn't intelligent, how could nature and the universe work the way it does? Would love be a part of a system that wasn't benevolent? Would the processes of life and birth in man, animal, and nature be so incredibly intricate and awesome? Does this sound like an energy that is unintelligent or has a negative intent? We could be that trillion to one evolutionary shot, but it seems logical that something more than accidental odds is occurring here. Even physicists who once dismissed any greater intelligence are now convinced of some intelligent force or higher power simply by the incredible nature of their discoveries and understanding about the universe we live in. This energy of "the unified field" has many names. Throughout history, it's been personified as "god." Unfortunately the word "god" has all sorts of preconceived concepts, rules, and associations that make me want to rap a nun's knuckles with a ruler. To be objective, I began referring to "the unified field" as "the Universal Life Force" or ULF. It is also called the Ground of Being, the Source, the Core Energy, the All That Is, X-Force, and the Oneness, to mention a few. These terms are interchangeable and mean basically the same thing—a positively-oriented phantasmagoric energetic field that animates and permeates everything. It is the Life Force that is the essence of our universe, and who knows how many other dimensions in the multiverse.

Enlightenment is an awakening to our true self. "Peak experiences" are a glimpse of that awakened self. If you've ever had a peak experience then you know something wild and wonderful is going on in the universe. These brief experiences of enlightenment can occur in the woods, on mountain tops, at the beach, or walking down the street. All of a sudden there's a shift in awareness and a feeling of incredible love, peace and joy and an understanding that is way beyond the ability of words to describe. There is a sense of oneness and connection to all people and things and a sense that this is right; that life as it is in this moment is the way it is supposed to be. If you have had this type of revelatory experience, then you know there is no question about the loving, benevolent, positive orientation of the Universal Live Force.

For those who have not had a peak experience, I cannot prove the existence of a benevolent universe; I can only report that a synthesis of spiritual wisdom, research, and anecdotal evidence indicates an intelligent, well intentioned, unified field exists. I daresay that the average person reading the same material would reach a similar conclusion. The unified field is not a person, judge, or gargantuan score keeper. It doesn't believe in guilt or sin. It doesn't think you are bad or in need of fixing. It doesn't care about how many times we swore or fantasized impure thoughts. It isn't interested in fear, punishment, and retribution. We made up all of that. It is simply a field of energy that is by its nature intelligent and loving. It is an energy that operates by the laws of physics and metaphysics, most of which we are just beginning to discover and understand.

You might ask, "If this Universal Life Force is so damn benevolent, why is all this stupidity and suffering going on?"

Well, there's this other funny thing called free will. We have free will to create whatever we please. The thought and feeling energies that we have interact with the creative force of the unified field and create themselves. Did you ever notice in a dream that whatever you think instantly appears? Supposedly, we manifest our physical reality the same way, by what we think and emote, except there is a big delay factor with the stuff forming in the physical world. We are often surprised at what we get because we create our reality at a deeper than conscious level. Our collective reality is formed by our collective consciousness. That's what shows up when we pool all of our individual thinking and emotional energies. There are some less-than-positive energies (such as fear) that contribute to forming the something-to-be-desired collective physical picture. It's like we all have a musical instrument in the symphony called earth, and we're still learning how to play.

Let's suppose, as these writings indicate, that we're part of a unified field, composed of a loving, benevolent energy. Being part of some awesome, positively oriented, intelligent energy seems like a good thing to me. It's clear it has nature handled pretty well and I'm a part of nature, at least as important as the trees. Why shouldn't this energy have me handled as well? Maybe, it does. Maybe everything is synchronistic and happening exactly as it should in conjunction with whatever we create for ourselves. Maybe we just don't see it—yet. Maybe our big brains just get in the way.

Really Good News

No sin, no blame, no fear.

Really Good News

THERE IS NO SIN. There is nothing to fear, nothing to worry about, or to defend against. What we understand to be God is an all loving energy that never judges and would never condemn anyone to an eternal hell. Just as a good parent would not condemn his or her children for making a mistake, why would we consider God to be any less compassionate then a kind parent? Remember the "judge not, least ye be judged" thing?

It, the ULF, God, the Ground of Being, the Source, the All That Is, the Big Enchilada, whatever you call it, is an unwavering energy of total love and peace with no concept of sin or judgment. "It" has no need to forgive because "It" has never condemned. It's not "Its" nature. We are already 'forgiven' because we were never condemned.

We, on the other hand, who made this place, employ our egos to judge like crazy, using judgment, guilt and fear to distract us from the truth of who we really are. Sin, if anything, is just a mistake, or as it's called in the bible, "harmartia," or, "missing the mark." It is straying from alignment with the ULF and the benefits that alignment brings. Lack of alignment, or "sin", brings its own natural consequences within the egocentric world of fear by what it attracts. It's not punishment, it's just physics, and the beauty of it is that there is nothing to be guilty about or defend against.

But, you say, there are bad people who do bad things. Yes, people do bad things, but everyone is the same Good God energy at their core. Many little lambs have lost their way and have done some very 'bad sheep' things. People will even punish themselves with guilt-induced illusory hells in this or other dimensions, but where hells exists they are made by man, not by the ULF. The ULF neither condemns nor punishes our dream world mistakes.

There may be some people who think that without having to fear God's retribution it would be okay to run amok. Personally, I'd advise against running amok. There is still this thing called karma, a.k.a. cosmic poetic justice. It's a mirror of what we need to see and learn from in order to return to alignment. It's not retribution either, it's just physics, so unless you want to be on the receiving end of the cosmic reaction to your own fear-based bad behavior it's best to treat everyone, including yourself, with compassion.

The Big Secret That Isn't

"We are already that which we seek."

– Unknown

The Big Secret That Isn't

YOU ARE ALREADY enlightened. That's right. Ninety-nine out of one hundred gurus agree that human beings are already enlightened. All the peace, joy, knowledge and power, everything you've imagined possible and much more, already exists inside of each of us. You have it. Our core, our inner-self, consciousness, being, essence, soul, light within, or whatever term you want to use, is already in a state of perfect peace and harmony. You are perfectly okay. There is nothing wrong with you. You are, in fact, already an enlightened being.

It seems that our essence is a piece of this universal consciousness that some call God. Since we are composed of this universal energy, we are part of, and connected to, the incredible love, creativity and power of this Universal Life Force. We have access to everything in its field. Are you starting to get the picture? If there is only one thing and we are part of it, then we have access to "All That Is," all the inherent love, knowledge, peace, power to create, and boundless adventure it has to offer. We have enlightenment—and we need do nothing to obtain what we already have.

"So how come I don't feel enlightened?" you ask. "How come I have no experience of inner peace and happiness?" Because we have so much stuff piled on top of it, we seldom, if ever, experience it. Unfortunately our minds and bodies contain so many barriers to our enlightened selves that we can't experience the daylight through the trees. We must peel back the layers of our ego personality and release emotional blockages in order to expose our enlightened centers.

That's the big secret. We've got this super conscious core, the real deal, but our access to it is blocked. Having the survival instincts and fears of the animal kingdom, plus the capacity for total love, peace, and enlightenment housed in the same physical form can make for some pretty interesting internal conversations. To understand the major barriers to the enlightened core, it is helpful to know something about the key players participating in our inner experience.

Basic Dimensions

"You can never cross the ocean unless you have the courage to lose sight of the shore."

– Christopher Columbus

Basic Dimensions

THREE DIFFERENT TYPES of dimensions exist within us. First, there is the enlightened self that we have been speaking of, also called our being, inner self, true self, core, soul, inner light, essence, or whatever you prefer.

Next, there is a mental dimension, usually led by the ego-brain, consisting of our thoughts, concepts, thinking, and beliefs.

Finally, the experiential dimension deals with our sensations, energies, and feelings that take place in the body. Thinking and feeling are very dissimilar occurrences within the same organism. One stimulates the other and vice-versa, but it's like comparing apples to carburetors; they are completely different.

Feelings have their own natural process. If they are allowed to follow their course, new learning and well-being occur, integrating the past with the present. Because most of us are uncomfortable feeling unpleasant emotions, we employ a number of techniques to avoid our experience of these emotions. We can tense our muscles, breathe incompletely, or go up into our heads and think. Hiding out in the thinking in our brains is a pervasive, even pathological, strategy we use to avoid emotions. Thinking feels safe because thinking doesn't feel. Brains are aware of the feelings, but the sensation occurs in the body.

Do you know what happens to the emotions we avoid? Unfelt feeling energies, or repressed feelings, remain in our bodies, waiting for us to experience them. They remain, emanating their not-fun-to-feel energy at a level not conscious to us, coloring the way we think, feel, and act. The problem is, these stored energies block the more enjoyable energies available to us in the present. They leave little or no room for the knowledge, love, and peace of the Universal Life Force to flow through us. We are blocked by the emotional refuse of the past and an overabundance of thinking. Ironically, simply feeling the emotions and sensations in our bodies can unblock them. Easier said than done, I know, yet harder and more unpleasant in the long run if left unfelt and unresolved.

thinking emotions feeling energies feelings self knowbodies sensations different avoid experience unpleasant present inner think body number consisting conscious simply experiential overabundance knowledge flow available heads stimulates use Finally repressed Universal Three remain Thinking occurs enjoyable enlightened past comparing pathological place go within dimension Hiding

Fear

"Death is just a change in life style."

—Stephen Levine

FEAR IS THE most common energetic block to our inner life force. Most of us have quite a bit of fear stored in our bodies because fear is not pleasant to experience, and it subconsciously reminds of us death. It's the original negative emotion that all other fear-based emotions are linked to.

Emotions work by association. That scary event reminds me of that other scary event which gets filed next to the previous scary event, etc. So all of our present day fears become associated with the mother of all original fears—our basic fear of not surviving. These ancient, instinctual fears that we share with our animal ancestors have been passed down through our cells, genes, and politicians to affect us even today. We also carry childhood "survival fears" into adulthood. These were created when a parent got angry at us and we feared they might not continue to care for us. Children are not physically or emotionally capable of coping with the intensity of fears of dying so they protect themselves by avoiding and therefore storing the emotion.

The result of habitually avoiding and repressing feelings is an uncomfortable experience of our body. Thankfully, these stored fears need only to be processed out of the body. According to bioenergetics and other body-oriented psycho-therapies, this means simply feeling the feelings. Experiencing the emotion releases the stored energy and its influence. The physics are simple. When we resist a feeling energy, it remains stuck in the body, continually and subtly affecting the way we think, feel, and act. If we fully experience our feelings, they run their course and are gone, leaving us relaxed, with a clearer channel for the ULF energies to flow through us.

On a psychological level, if you want to be emotionally healthy, you have to be willing to feel your emotions. Being comfortable with the experience in your body, including feelings and fear, is essential to the ability to feel good, and have a positive life experience. On a spiritual level, if you block your feelings, you also block the ULF. Both are sensations of energies we experience in our bodies. Peace, love, compassion, creativity, and knowledge are some of the energetic properties of the ULF. They are characteristics, or attributes of the ULF that originate from our non-physical self, beyond the body. We experience these attributes of the Life Force through the body, so if we have lost access to the experience of our body, we have also lost access to our experience of the ULF within us. In other words, the ability to experience feelings is essential in order to remain unblocked, and therefore able to experience the more subtle energies of the ULF and the benefits those energies can bring.

For people who are comfortable with their feelings, the body is generally a pleasant place to be and experience of the ULF is accessible.

Other people have an excess of stored emotional material from their past clogging up the works. For those who chronically avoid feelings, basic access to experience may need to be cultivated through affirming willingness to feel emotions or possibly undergo psychotherapy (See Appendix A: Processing Feelings). Unfelt or unresolved emotions from the past can then be resolved to make the body a comfortable place to be and a clearer channel for the ULF. It's not called psycho-spirituality for nothing. This is the psychological component that many spiritual seekers tend to overlook, thinking they can just affirm, think, or will their way to spiritual bliss. Spiritual techniques are important and useful but cannot replace the basic psychological groundwork needed for emotional and spiritual health.

The Ego

Life is an experience, not a stream of thoughts in your head.

The Ego

YOU MAY HAVE noticed something—thinking about life is not the same as living it.

Life is an experience, not a thought. But try and tell that to the ego.

Another roadblock on the highway to heaven is the ego's propensity to promote fear primarily because its continued existence depends on it. The ego is a holographic picture we have of ourselves that lives in our brains. The ego is a powerful, alive, and useful concept of ourselves we use for operating in physical reality. We develop an image of ourselves in our brain that has all the attributes, attitudes, and appearances we think are necessary to get what we think we want or need. The funny thing (not ha-ha funny either) is that the ego thinks it *is* who we are. It is not. Thoughts and thinking are not who we are.

The irony is we really are the Universal Life Force. We are this point of light or consciousness/awareness that is part of and dancing in the Unified Field. The problem is we're usually not dancing. We're more likely sitting in the corner, thinking. In fact, we've been up in our heads thinking we are this thought form of a person for so long, we've deluded ourselves into thinking that really *is* who we are! Not so.

Check it out. Stop thinking for a second. Did you disappear? No, you're still here. Who or what is that behind your thinking?

When we start to move inward to experience our spiritual self, the ego gets worried. The ego, being this collection of thoughts, attributes, concepts, and images that exists in the mental realm, knows nothing about the experience of our true Self. As we move inward, the ego becomes afraid for its survival (and ours), because it thinks it is who and what we are. The ego has no understanding of the real you, the non-physical energy-being that you are. To your ego, you are walking off the edge of the earth (which in a way, you are). Fearing for its (and your) survival, it does everything possible to distract you from the journey inward towards what it believes is death. How ironic, when in reality we are returning home to our more natural state.

The ego uses fear to keep us engrossed in its reality of separation and deprivation.

It keeps us occupied, thinking about the past and the future in our brain, away from our experience of the present moment, which just happens to be our access point to the greater reality of the ULF.

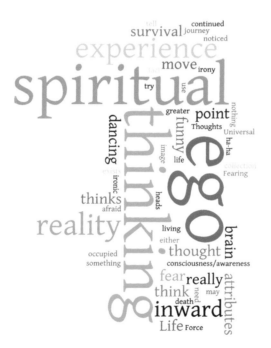

Nothing to Fear

Bodies die, we don't.

Nothing to Fear

DEATH OF THE physical body is inevitable. Nobody gets off the planet alive. We spend a lot of time distracted and suffering with survival-based fears, instigated and promoted by the ego, blocking the experience of our true self. Imagine what your experience would be like without such a primal fear.

I once saw pictures of Buddhist monks walking back and forth on a path with a skeleton hanging on each end of the walkway. I wondered what kind of sick religion this was until I discovered they were meditating on the inevitability of the death of the physical body. Buddhists confront this survival fear head on. The truth is, we don't survive; at least our bodies don't, and there's absolutely nothing we can do about it. We might extend or prolong our lives somewhat, but eventually, we all leave this world.

We can begin to release our fear of death by accepting its inevitability and by asking ourselves what is to be gained by fearing something that we can't control or stop. Does it make any sense? Do we get anything out of fearing death? Of course an immediate fear of being run down by a speeding car can spare your life for the short term, but we're not talking about that. We're referring to an ever-present core fear of annihilation, a fear of ceasing to exist, that is the root of all our other fears. Is there any benefit from fearing something that can't be controlled? If it is truly inevitable, it will happen no matter what, and your fear will not change anything. (That's what inevitable means.) If you fear the inevitable, you gain only fear.

We will still need to experience and release our stored fears as we live and grow. We will still have our innate and useful survival fears of speeding cars. At the same time, we can learn to live with less fear, and eventually without fear, by accepting the truth about our fears and ourselves.

The fear that you are going to die is based on two misperceptions. One is that you have some control over the death of your physical body. The other is that your entire being ceases to exist. The truth is, you really don't have a choice, and you don't cease to exist. The physical version of you will die, but fortunately, not the real you. Bodies come and go and someday your body will go. It simply helps to remember that you are not your body—bodies die; we don't.

The Unknown Dimension

"Reality is merely an illusion, albeit a very persistent one."

—Albert Einstein

The Unknown Dimension

OUR NATURAL STATE is that of an eternal, energetic, non-physical being. We don't die. The body dies but you're not just a body. The ego is a concept of yourself that animates and structures the body. It is identified with the body, and therefore naturally fears its end.

Supposedly, Freud discovered that the subconscious has no concept of death. He didn't realize the importance of what he had uncovered because it didn't fit into his framework. The subconscious does not conceive of death because the subconscious doesn't die.

It's one thing to say we originate in a non-physical dimension, but if we can't remember what it's like without a body, then it's crazy scary to think about going there. This is where it gets dicey for your ego, which doesn't want to hear about this and is going to do its best to convince you that it's total nonsense.

In our natural and original state we are spirit, not physical beings. Our individual ego has created our individual body. Our collective ego has created this physical dimension. Like a movie on the big screen, this dimension appears real. We arrive here, we lose access to our greater reality, we forget who and what we are, and where we come from.

Thankfully, our bodies may be separated but our spirit selves are not entirely disconnected. As eternal "divine sparks" of the ULF we have nothing to fear. "How," you might say, "can there be nothing to fear? Even if I'm some eternal spirit being, people die and suffer in this world." Imagine a movie. People appear to die yet do not. "But," you say, "movies aren't real." Imagine being a three-dimensional being (human) that can enter a two-dimensional reality (such as PlayStation) to experience things you want to and might not be able to in your normal 3-D existence. Now, imagine being a forth dimensional being and for your entertainment and education you can choose to enter a three-dimensional reality to experience things more intensely, or differently, than your non-physical dimension allows. It's like a playground, a physical holographic movie where, for the players, all seems real, yet in reality, when the game is over, you return to your natural state unharmed by the illusions you experienced.

Welcome to Reality.

The ego hangs on to the physical stuff, acquiring things, people, power, sex, and stuffed animals, because it helps alleviate the fear that the ego created in the first place. Quite a clever, one even might say, diabolical system. The ego creates a problem that doesn't exist and then engages us in resolving what cannot be resolved.

The fact is, we are going to have to give it all up anyway. We are going to lose our bodies and access to this dimension. We are going to return to a non-physical dimension, unfamiliar to us from this vantage point, yet, in truth, it's not unknown. We've been there many times. We just don't remember.

Ever had a dream in which you knew you were dreaming and could control what happens? It's called conscious or lucid dreaming. Good stuff. Your imagination is the only limit. Supposedly, the importance of meditation is learning how to control the mind and focus attention. These skills allow you to better navigate the non-physical dimensions. It's like a fantasy come true—peace, love, and the ability to go anywhere, and do anything you can imagine. Sound like fun?

Sounds like heaven.

Beliefs

"All that we are is the result of what we have thought. The mind is everything. What we think we become."

—Buddha

Beliefs

QUANTUM PHYSICS HAS caused a major shift in science. In old school physics everything had defined edges. It was all about particles. Quantum physicists have discovered something radically different. Everything exists both as waves of energy and possibly solid particles. The most astounding thing is that the energy of a wave becomes solid when it's observed. Wow.

Science is coming full circle to what the spiritualist and metaphysicians have been saying for a long time. We actually think physical reality into existence. You become what you believe.

What you believe is actually a "thought form" that provides the framework for the energy in the unified field to collect around. The thought forms of your beliefs structure the energy of the ULF and bingo – they create themselves just like events in a conscious dream. The difference is that things are much slower to form in the physical world and there's that pesky collective consciousness to deal with, as well. The beliefs we're talking about are the subconscious, deeply held, what some call "core" beliefs that are constantly influencing the unified field. These are not the daily conscious beliefs or thoughts such as, "I like chocolate pudding." Core beliefs define the quality of your life.

Core beliefs, especially those regarding your self-worth, determine what you experience. If you have subconscious, self-deprecating beliefs they will limit you, big time. Besides having the basic ability to experience your feelings, there is nothing as important as self-esteem and learning to love yourself, (or at least like yourself). Beliefs such as "I'm no good," or "I'm bad," or "I'm undeserving because I'm too short, tall, wide, poor, homely, or flatulent" will simply get in the way of you loving yourself. If deep down you don't believe you are worth loving, you're not going to welcome good feelings in your life. Your ability to have an enjoyable and satisfying life will be drastically diminished. Spiritually, your ability to experience love and the other positive attributes of the ULF will be blocked.

Maybe you're intrigued by the idea that we can influence our reality. Maybe you are one of the many people who are trying to "create your reality," using spiritual and quantum laws to actively manifest the content of your life. If so, be aware that undeserving, low self-worth beliefs are major barriers to any manifestation efforts you undertake. They can determine what you get and don't get in life. Believing you are unworthy or that you are not good enough will conflict with any efforts you may make at visualizing and manifesting positive results in the physical structure. Simply stated, you will not get 'good' results if you don't believe that you deserve good things.

Fortunately, core beliefs regarding self esteem can be changed. A little effort can result in profound and positive changes. (See Appendix B: Changing Beliefs Process.)

Manifesting

"The challenge is to believe your dreams in the center of the illusion."

—Emmanuel-Pat Rodegast

Manifesting

"You create your reality."
"You can manifest whatever you want."
"You, too, can be a millionaire."

P OP SPIRITUALITY IS SELLING what people want to hear. While technically true, the fine print is usually omitted. If creating your own reality was as simple as advertised, most of us would have won the lottery by now. So, how come we don't get what we want? It's the all-important subtleties that can cause failed efforts, disappointment, resignation, and suffering. What I've learned may not guarantee success, but at least you will have a better chance at creating the life you want, and hopefully, you'll become aware enough not to punish yourself if you don't get what you're trying to create.

Affirmations are a prime example of a manifestation technique in need of clarification. Affirmations are a common manifestation technique of simply repeating a new belief or statement of what you want with the idea it will interact with the Unified Field and create itself. However, these conscious statements have little chance of working if deeper contrary beliefs are present. For example, if I believe deep down that I am unworthy as a person then affirmations for attracting wealth will conflict with my undeserving beliefs, and my efforts will fail.

First, a person needs to become aware of any deeper contrary beliefs. Repeating an affirmation does have the benefit of bringing the less-than-conscious beliefs to the surface if you simply listen to the reaction in your mind. This makes them available to work with and change. Once you've uncovered contradictory or core beliefs in need of revision, the psycho-therapeutic technology to change beliefs is available. It can be used to enhance self esteem and your ability to consciously manifest what you desire. (See Appendix B: Changing Beliefs Process.)

One nuance in manifestation methodology is a seeming contradiction. Intrinsic in wanting something is that what you "want" is something you don't yet have. The act of wanting can affirm two things. The two thoughts within "wanting" are A: that you don't have whatever is it is you want (why else would you want it), and B: that you want to have it. If you do what most of us do and focus on B, you usually miss that A can also be going on, and that is actually affirming you don't have it. Physics of the Field are simple. If you put A into the Field (that you don't have), you'll get not having it.

The same dynamics operate on an energetic level. Really wanting some-thing is often really not wanting something. An emotional reaction or upset around what you don't want can become the underlying energy that gets repeatedly focused on and manifested. "I hate how large my head is," or "I'm upset that I don't have enough money," are expressions of the emotional upset about how poor I am, or how huge my head is. This perpetuates the energetic thought forms of inadequate funds and head girth. Unconsciously the focus is on the self deprecating emotions and in essence saying "I am upset that I'm not rich" so you are actually affirming "I'm not rich." Oops. Acceptance or acknowledgement of your present situation is a more useful starting point. It's better to first feel and release any emotional upsets. This places you in your experience of the present where the true power to create exists. Accept the way things are and then have the intention and imagery of what is desired.

It is important to be aware of the words, emotions and intentions involved. Better than saying "I want" would be understanding and knowing that what you want is already being created and is forming as you visualize and speak it. Try "being" that which you desire. Use the "I am" statement. Try visualizing or experiencing what it is like to be in the desired state. Try gratitude. It is the energy of "thank you for having." That's a good place to be if you're creating having something and very different from wanting out of not having it. Basically, it's about imagining yourself already having or being whatever it is you wish to manifest. This seems to contradict logic and the accepted linear concept of how things work, but in the dynamics of creation the chicken and the egg are one. Eventually, the physical catches up to the creation of the mental thought forms.

A great deal of metaphysical literature asserts that we are responsible for creating everything in our lives. It may be true on some level, but it's more realistic to consider that there is some structure to the collective consciousness we live in. As a middle aged guy who can't jump, I don't think I have a shot at manifesting being an NBA basketball star. Technically, it may be true that we are responsible for every aspect of the creation of our lives but as a practical matter we have signed on with the shared physical reality and we are subject to its framework. As a result, I haven't seen many people manifest winning the lottery and most of them end up creating disappointment and suffering instead.

People commonly feel like a failure if what they consciously try to manifest doesn't happen. Because a person's effort to manifest the Powerball jackpot doesn't work, it doesn't mean that they are a failure. Maybe deep down they really don't believe they will succeed. Maybe that person hasn't cleared beliefs that have become blockages. Maybe the goal is too big to start with. Maybe the person on this earthly level doesn't see the big picture and it's not what they really need, or it's not in alignment with their greater purpose. Like those masters of rock and roll said, "You can't always get what you want, but if you try sometimes you might find you get what you need."

Actually, trying is not needed. The physics of the positively-oriented source energy will naturally attract to you what you truly need, even if it's not consciously what you want. Simply stated—all you need to do is accept your current reality, align with the ULF, and have faith it will bring you what you need, and maybe even what you want.

If you want, you can choose to gently guide your life within this structure. If this is an endeavor you wish to pursue, I want to impress upon you two things regarding the subject.

First, undeserving beliefs are often overlooked barriers that will require your attention if you are to be successful.

Second, everything, including your good self, is okay just the way it is, even if you're not as successful as you want to be in manifesting what you think you want.

Create Your Reality vs.
Let Go, Let the ULF

"If you want others to be happy, practice compassion. If you want to be happy, practice compassion."

—14th Dalai Lama

Create Your Reality vs. Let Go, Let the ULF

THERE APPEARS TO be two divergent approaches to the "getting what you want" game.

On one hand, you have the "how to create your own reality" method we have been talking about, and on the other, we have the "Let go, let God" approach. Should we actively manifest, or trust that we will get what we truly need?

We have free will. We can choose to do either, or neither. When we do neither, we are still continually unconsciously creating our reality out of our ego and in conjunction with the collective reality (among other influences). It just happens. It's just the physics of the way things work.

We also have the option to take an active role in consciously steering and creating our physical reality within this structure, at least to some extent. It's our choice. Go ahead and see if you can manifest a big house, more money, or a smaller head. There's "no blame" as the Buddhists say, no penalty, no sin involved. The fundamental lessons and the ULF are always there awaiting our return. Like *A Course in Miracles* says, the lesson is mandatory; you just decide when to do it.

We usually create what our egos think we need, as opposed to what we really need. Our egos think we need lots of money, possessions, and personal care products to defend against death. Ironically, ultimately, we are eternal beings and already have the security that we seek. We don't know the whole story (of what we are here to learn and do), but the alternative to not knowing is having faith in what does. We can choose to let go, let the ULF. We can decide to consciously align with the Universal Life Force and accept and trust in its course.

You may have noticed, the ULF frequently offers a different direction than does our egos. The lessons of the core energy within us are concerned with learning of Its Love and Peace, not about fear and defense. The good news is that the positive orientation of the ULF is always moving us, or trying to move us, in a positive love and growth direction regardless of the muddy and fearful interface of the ego. It does this "each to his or her own measure," within the structure we have chosen, consciously or unconsciously.

As we mature spiritually, we understand more, and the desires of the ego lessen. We accept that our egos don't know what's best. We begin to understand that our inner Self does, and all that we truly need is available for us when we let go. We have faith that the ULF is going to bring us what we need. We move from ego-centered awareness to the ability to experience more deeply, to listen to the ULF, and to operate from its guidance. We let the Universal Life Force lead us in positive directions, and to the creations we need to participate in. Eventually, the need for identification with our ego lessens and we identify with the ULF and become one with the Enlightenment that is our essence.

Being vs. Thinking

"If you want to be happy, be."

—Tolstoy

Being vs. Thinking

THERE IS AN entirely different way of operating in the world. It is based more on the "let go, let God" approach rather than the incessant thinking of the ego. It consists of experiencing life in the present moment, rather than thinking about it. It is "being" rather than thinking. It works by choosing to be in the experience of your body. For many, being, or living in the "now", as Tolle describes it, is difficult to achieve. Difficult, because the experience of the present means experiencing the sensations in the body, and for many the body is uncomfortable due to stored emotions (see Fear). This often overlooked barrier to the present inhibits many people from being able to "be" in the present. Once a person becomes friendly with their feelings, it becomes easier to stay in the present with the experience of self.

Our experience (rather than our thinking) is the portal for the larger reality. Being and trusting in the positive nature of the ULF naturally enhances the ability of the ULF to bring us what we truly need. Being vs. thinking will result in a more relaxed and different way of living life from what we are used to. Most of the time, it seems like we have to plan and think in order to live. It's not always realistic or possible to let go of our thinking to just "be", especially at first. The idea is to start to play in this new space, to just gently increase the amount of time we spend in our experience, living out of our "beingness."

Being offers some interesting benefits. In this state there is awareness of the body and a greater potential for experiencing love and peace, two things which are usually absent with ego-centered thinking. With "being" there is access to the larger awareness of the ULF, a significant aspect of which is organic thought. Organic thoughts are different from ego-based thinking. If thoughts originate from your ego in your head they have a different quality than if they originate from your physical experience of self and your being.

Try and notice the difference between the origin and qualities of these two different types of brain activity. Ego thinking is more of an ongoing, time oriented process of the ego's machinations trying to fix the past or future. It is like a magician's patter, diverting your attention from experiencing yourself and from seeing what is really going on. "Blah, blah, blah, look at this, look at that, isn't this exciting," or "You did that to me," and "Maybe if I review this ten times in my head it will change the feelings it generates that I'm trying to avoid." You know, wacky ego stuff.

Being produces a wholly different brain experience. Organic thoughts are more like impressions, knowledge, or awareness that rise naturally from the experience of self. They are often sense impressions with more of an "Oh, that's it," realization quality, not the active thinking and puzzling the ego does. Allowing thoughts to flow from our being is like having access to the infinite "hard drive" of the universe versus the limited "random access memory" of the ego.

Initially, organic thoughts may appear to be slower than ego thinking, but the breadth and quality are far superior. I admit the distinction is subtle, especially at first, but the difference is real, and it represents a radical and beneficial shift in our consciousness. Radical, not because it's new, but because most of us have become entrenched in living out of our ego mind. Revolutionary because it promises to provide us far greater access to who we are and to the benefits that alignment with self brings.

Being vs. Doing

"You need not do anything. Remain sitting at your table and listen. You need not even listen, just wait. You need not even wait, just learn to be quiet, still and solitary. And the world will freely offer itself to you unmasked. It has no choice, it will roll in ecstasy at your feet."

—Franz Kafka from his poem,

"Learn to Be Quiet."

Being vs. Doing

DOING OUT OF being vs. doing out of doing. There's a big difference.

There's a lot of doing for the sake of doing, stemming from a neurotic need to do. The doing in itself is not in question; it's where the motivation to do originates. A large amount of doing is the busy work of egoville. Sure, doing things is necessary to maintain us in this dimension, but it's worth knowing the difference between the neurotic doing, driven by the ego, and doing that flows from being.

Doing for doing's sake is the ego's frenetic dance. Like a gunslinger shooting at the feet of his terrorized victim, the ego keeps you jumping. It keeps you distracted and occupied with incessant activity, glitz, and drama. Why? For its preservation; so you forget who you are and your ability to choose another modus operandi—being in your experience of the ULF.

Ego doing is often the preoccupation with our need to accomplish and acquire in order to be okay with ourselves and to validate our existence.

The ego preys on our undeserving beliefs and having to do things in order to be worthy.

In reality we're in good with the ULF (because we are It), and we need to do nothing to be okay. We are intrinsically worthy of good things and don't need to do anything for that to be true.

Action that arises out of being is the Buddhist concept of "right action." It is trusting that engaging the ULF through the simple act of being will bring the awareness of the right action to take. Imagine "doing" that rises out of an internal place of being relaxed in the moment, trusting that what you need to do will naturally occur to you. Imagine knowing that action will bring you what you need. Wouldn't it be great if your experience of simply being in the present moment provides you with what you truly need ?

It's hard for most of us to believe it is possible to live this way, but there is nothing to stop us from experimenting with being and then doing. What's going to bring you a better life experience—action born of fearful thinking or relaxed openness? With egoic fear-based thinking you tend to see, do, and attract fearful things out of your possible life experiences. Being connected to the larger love and peace-based self has a much higher likelihood of providing you with the "right action" needed to guide your life in a positive direction.

For a bonus gift, it's a gateway to another dimension. It's the access point to experience the Greater Reality from whence we came, the ULF, the Field, and All That Is. With that connection you have a much better chance of receiving what you need and desire and infinitely more.

Acceptance

"Always say 'yes' to the present moment. What could be more futile, more insane, than to create inner resistance to what already is? What could be more insane than to oppose life itself, which is now and always now? Surrender to what is. Say 'yes' to life—and see how life suddenly starts working for you rather than against you."

—Eckhart Tolle

Acceptance

IT IS WHAT IT IS. Non-acceptance is wanting it to be some way other than what it is.

But it is the way it is. Non-acceptance doesn't change what is.

If you don't accept "what is" and you resist the present moment, your mind engages in struggle, and you lose your self into "ego world." You also reduce your access to information and your best course of action.

Acceptance should not be confused with resignation. It is not giving up. It is not saying, "do nothing." It is saying that there are benefits when you accept, then act, as opposed to action that springs from non-acceptance.

The fact is, you can't get somewhere else without being here first. There is no real power to change what is happening in reality from outside of reality. Being here, in the moment, is where reality exists. This is the only place where effective action can be taken.

Being in reaction to something in your mind brings you somewhere else, to a place that doesn't really exist as anything except a thought, "ego land," resulting in struggle and dissatisfaction.

Ask yourself, "What is the benefit to not accepting what is?" Resistance? Aggravation? Struggling to decide what action to take? Thinking? What kind of thinking? Where does it come from? Ego thinking and organic thought can both result in action, but which has the potential to bring a more advantageous course of action?

Non-acceptance = reactive thinking = ego land. It evokes a narrow, ego-based thinking process, limited and motivated by fear. Bottom line: non-acceptance usually doesn't move you forward. Your ego gets a boost, but as the little Jedi guy says, "Lost you are."

Acceptance gains you entrance to a different state of being and a thought process that works with what is, opening us to information accessed from a larger field of information and creativity. Action that stems from acceptance instead of reaction has a far greater potential for positive consequences. It grounds you in the only state you truly have the power to change and it avoids "monkey mind" mania.

Without acceptance we often get into "stories." Stories can become a place in our ego-mind that we live out of, effectively becoming a substitute for reality. A story is not your experience of your life. It is a collection of words describing or complaining or judging, but it is not you. We tell ourselves and others stories about our reaction, why it's justified, why we're right, why another wrong, and who's to blame.

These stories become justifications for one ego to feel better than another, and a host of other psychological payoffs on the on ramp to egoville. These stories can be repeated so often they become entrenched. They can develop a life of their own and take us farther away from the lives we wish to lead. Stories can even develop into complex energetic "thought forms" that can be hard to let go.

This is an opportunity to practice acceptance of what is and experience any feelings the story may be helping you avoid. Try forgiving yourself and others. Meditate. Ask for inner guidance. Sometimes, stories become so fixed in your psyche you may need to seek professional guidance. That's right, the "T" word: therapy. As scary as that may sound, it's almost always enjoyable and life enhancing!

One more thing about stories in your head. If you start living out of a story then that story interacts with the energy field and contributes to your life creation. So, if you're going to have a story, don't have it be about what you don't have and why you don't have it. Have your story be about the good things you like and want for yourself and others.

Forgiveness

"In your brother is the light. See him as sinless, and there can be no fear in you."

—A Course in Miracles

Forgiveness

ACCORDING TO THE *Course in Miracles,* there are only two types of expression: love, and the cry for love. We cry out for love when we are afraid and separated from our Source. Some emotions are so powerful our bodies are not energetically capable of handling them. Sometimes we're just not ready or willing to experience them. In these situations the cry for love often takes the form of blame, the opposite of forgiveness.

When we attack or blame others it is nearly always a projection, or subconscious shifting onto others of the emotions we don't want to experience like fear or guilt. "I'm feeling lost in fear and I'm crying out for love," turns into: "You are to blame for my fear-based feelings and if I can convince myself this is true I won't have to feel them." The other person's ego then responds defensively and attacks in return, generating more fear. Without forgiveness we fall into this endless fearful egoic cycle of attack and defend.

Forgiveness is responding with love. Forgiveness avoids the attack trap of our ego and brings us home to the love we share at our core with our attacker. Forgiveness is seeing ourselves and others as spiritual beings who have strayed from their spiritual center and are in need of love. It is remembering to "forgive them for they know not what they do."

Forgiveness acknowledges that fear, guilt, blame, and attack result from mistakenly judging ourselves and others to have sinned (see The Really Good News). It is taking into account that we are all lost sheep on this bus, and accepting and forgiving people for their apparent digressions. It acknowledges that their apparent digressions are just that, apparent, and, in reality, not actually significant because they are unreal apparitions of the ego-produced physical dream.

According to *A Course in Miracles,* a lack of forgiveness is based on the misperception that one person can hurt another. The truth is we ultimately can't really be hurt, because we are eternal energetic beings. Even hurtful, physically damaging events in this physical dimension, including death, have no lasting affect on our true self, on our true spirit life in the ULF. This can be especially hard to comprehend, especially when it involves apparently big hurts and transgressions. To make it even more difficult, the ego fights this threatening concept to its death. You can expect ego-induced, emotional ups and downs for daring to think it true.

Forgiveness is easier said than sincerely done, but if you're interested in understanding the mechanics of forgiving at a life altering level, *A Course in Miracles* is worth the effort. If you want to try turning your cheek with forgiveness, start with forgiving yourself and practice with less emotionally charged situations. The payoff is avoiding the painful pit of ego mania while increasing time within the ULF and your experience of understanding and peace. Most of all, practicing acceptance and forgiveness helps to bring us home to who and what we are: an eternal, super-conscious aspect of the positively oriented Universal Life Force with nothing to fear or defend against.

All is Sweetness and Light
—yeah right

"If you're going through hell, keep going."

—Churchill

All is Sweetness and Light
—yeah right

AT THE CORE of my being I'm just as enlightened as the next person. I'm also just as removed from my experience of enlightenment most of the time. I'm an average person with research skills and the ability to explain things. I'm working, paying bills, and to the extent I can, learning and applying what I've learned. Honestly, much of the time, it doesn't feel like, "It's all good."

Most of our daily experience is not all peace, love, and enlightenment. Even though the ground of being is good, and the ever-present ULF assures that there's really nothing to fear, the ego keeps reengaging us in the illusion. We continually lapse back into the dream of the ego and suffering and separation.

On top of that, we have to deal with the emotional ups and downs caused by the growth cycles of learning. We naturally evolve and learn, and sometimes that means painful experiences and uncomfortable feelings. At times it's not easy. At times, it's really hard, even awful. But the teachings of these spiritual masters who understood the nature of reality help point us in the right direction. If the Ground of Being is a totally supportive Life Force and we are eternal energy beings temporarily living in a physical dreamscape, then there is really nothing to fear.

Remembering that can have a considerable impact.

By choosing to remember that the ULF is at our core and that everything is ultimately okay, life is far less scary. This awareness will help us live through difficult times of pain and suffering. It becomes okay to experience and release fearful events and, soon enough, find ourselves enjoying life once again. We will increasingly experience more peace, satisfaction, and well-being. With this knowledge of the ULF we can increase the time we spend in our true self and in being relaxed and confident in our ULF-guided experience of life.

The Path

"Don't Worry, Be Happy."

—Meher Baba

The Path

LET'S RECAP. There's no gain in fearing inevitable physical death or the unknown. You are not annihilated. It's just another dimension. The Ground of Being is eternal and positively-oriented. The ULF has us completely handled so there's nothing to defend against, no need to tense our bodies and avoid our experience. Who we are lives on in the next dimension, one of many to explore. Learn to trust the ULF and live in its field. Relax, enjoy the experience of life to the extent you are able. Experience and be in the present.

"But how do I make that happen?" you ask.

The ability to experience life is an essential attribute to living and enjoying life, not just spiritual growth. The goal is simply, gently, to go there more often, slowly increasing your ability to remain in an experience of yourself rather than your ego thinking. For most people it will take time and practice. Be compassionate with your good self. It's about gradually increasing your time away from egoville.

Being in the experience of the present naturally allows for feelings to surface, including old feelings from the past. If access to your experience is limited or denied, then your priority is making friends with feelings. (See Appendix-A.)

Being friends with emotions entails understanding that repressed feelings are only unpleasant sensations. These avoided feelings make the body an uncomfortable place to be and simply need to be felt so that they can be released. This creates a clearer channel to experience the peace and love that exists at our core. In situations where regaining access to emotions or releasing emotions is especially difficult there is always psychotherapy.

Beyond learning to live centered in your experience, you may choose to accelerate your journey inward to your enlightened center by doing some type of psycho-spiritual practice. There's practicing acceptance and forgiveness. Breathing exercises and meditations connect us to our experience in the present moment. Mindfulness meditation is being aware, focusing on your experience of yourself as you move through life. Chi Kung utilizes the mind's ability to move energy through the body to clear blockages and heal. Buddhist compassion meditation is remembering to feel compassion for yourself and then others (you can't give what you don't have so give it to yourself first). The idea is to look for something that is easy and enjoyable that works for you. No fear. Relax, take it easy, take your time, and go gently.

You have a choice between spending your time in ego land or in a space defined by love and aligned with the ULF. The Hindu yogis talk about "auto-suggestion." It's not their divine recommendation for a new car. "Auto" means self. The idea is suggesting to yourself rather than responding automatically to the constant suggestions we receive from our senses, the body, and the ego. It's a reminder that you should take charge and choose. For example, if you had a choice, would you rather be the ocean or a raft floating on it? The beauty of it is, that in reality, we are the ocean, not the raft. Choose the ocean; otherwise the ego chooses the raft.

We're not going to be able to do away with the ego, nor could we while we live on this planet. We use the ego to navigate this dimension, but it is an advantage and a gift, to be able to choose to not be controlled by it. You can let go, let God, but you still need to choose to let go. If you don't, the ego will choose in the absence of your choosing, and you will revolve on the cycle of incarnations. That's fine, it doesn't hurt. No blame. Eventually, we tire of this playground and listen to the inner calling to return home and continue our internal journey.

When people move deeper and look at the space within, they are often startled by what at first glance appears to be a vast and empty void. This nothingness or emptiness, as the Buddhists call it, is not completely empty. It is a subtle field of energy, the fabric of the universe. It is the unified field that our consciousness is part of, is at one with, and interacts with, to create physical and non-physical states.

No wonder the ego is afraid. Your growth and movement toward your true self is like asking the ego to do a space walk with no lifeline. It stimulates fear. It says you are going to die. But, there are no reported cases of people dying from feeling their emotions or exploring internal space. In times of fear it can help to remind yourself that fears' message is untrue. It may feel like you're going to die, but you won't. You just want to be able to pick and choose whether you are going to operate out of your ego or your being. You want it to be okay to explore this inner world, which you know is safe (it's' got the ULF seal of approval), and return to the ego-based operations as needed.

Unfortunately, like the Chinese finger traps, the more you try to wrestle and change things within the ego's structure, the more embroiled you become in its convoluted substitute for reality. It deludes us into thinking that resisting and figuring things out will somehow change the past or the future for the better. It does not. The solution? Do an end run around the wacky ego thing. Choose to focus on something better.

Remember the Unconditionally Loving Force at our core. It has everything handled. There is nothing to fear. We are eternal spirit.

Remember to Remember

Choose or the ego chooses for you.

Remember to Remember

REMEMBER TO REMEMBER. Remember to choose. It's a simple path.

How much effort does it take to choose?

An effortless effort.

Choose to return to that understanding of our true nature and positively-oriented core as often as you can remember.

Remind yourself of the unconditional nature of the Love that resides in you, that is, in fact, who and what you are.

Choose your experience of being in the present rather than the thinking swirling in your head.

Remember to choose or the ego chooses for you.

Choose the Universal Life Force.

Remember to have compassion for yourself and others.

Remember to remember.

Choose to align with the love-based reality. Breathe in love and light. Remember what the Buddhist's call "the View," the sum of our entire understanding of the positive nature of the Ground of Being. Choose to be in your experience of whatever representation of the ULF works for you—Love, the Ground of Being, your new, improved understanding of God, whatever brings you Home into your experiential Self.

Remember the ULF and you are One, and It has everything handled. There is nothing to fear. You can relax.

Could it really be that all we need to do is remember to choose? Could it be … ?

It's a real knee-slapper, folks. You know how many of us are in the spiritual trenches, working our auras to a beady little line, trying to experience our enlightened self, achieve nirvana or whatever our version of spiritual completion is? What a paradox. All that effort isn't necessary. In fact, it is largely counterproductive. How ironic that the path to enlightenment requires little to no effort. Instead, it requires an effortless effort, a lack of struggle. It requires choosing.

We are that which we seek. We are already that which we desire in our greatest dream of love. Thanks be to G.O.D.—the growth-oriented and directed positive nature of the Unified Field. Due to man's inner connection to It we are perfectly okay just the way we are!

We need only trust and relax in the Flow. It is our heritage. It is who and what we are. We are naturals. So, like the guru says, "Don't worry, be happy."

Our understanding that the ULF has us completely taken care of deepens as we begin to let go into the flow more often and more completely. We accept and experience the life force that is at our core. We understand that when we leave this dimension we will rejoin a non-physical one where there is no separation from the love and no limits. We live life knowing there is nothing to fear. Isn't that what we all truly want, what we are always really striving for—that love, that peace, that greater reality we sense inside of us? Isn't that what we really are? Isn't that what we really want to be and experience? Could it be as simple as remembering to remember?

Final Note

THE WEBSITE www.EnlightenmentMadeSimple.info has research, links, stories, books, and information to help you explore and deepen your experience of the Life Force. If you found this field guide useful and think others may as well, please help disseminate this information by visiting the website. Consider purchasing copies of *Enlightenment* for people who might be in need of the information.

All proceeds from Internet sales go to support the dissemination of this material through the website and the ultimate creation of a documentary film on the topics it contains. Ten percent of profits are given to the Heifer Project and Amnesty International. (Even if the world is a strikingly realistic movie, it still helps to have compassion for those suffering in a dream.)

Remember to remember.

Appendices

Appendix A – Processing Feelings

IF YOU WANT to experience your true self and the benefits that brings, then you must have access to your experience.

If you are one of the many people who are out of touch with their feelings, or your access to experience is limited, gaining that access is your first priority.

Here is some information to get you started. Begin with a willingness to feel by repeatedly affirming to yourself, "I am willing to feel the sensations in my body." Without that willingness it isn't going to happen. This ability is so basic and important that a psychologist and I wrote a handbook specifically to help people to access their feelings. Regaining lost access to emotions, how to process feelings, and learning to love self is all detailed in "The Human Operators Manual – How Feelings Work: A Psychological Primer." (Available at www.EnlightenmentMadeSimple.com.) Learning to regain access to lost feelings can take time and practice but it is essential. There is no personal growth or emotional well-being if you can't feel your feelings.

Some people have access to feelings, but their experience of their body is still uncomfortable because of repressed emotions. If you have an excess of fear-based emotions you have not released, then focusing away from the ego is much more difficult. These stored emotions are easily restimulated by the ego for its own purposes and are barriers to deeper experience. Repressed fear can process out slowly over time, or lifetimes, but if you want to actively release them from your body, here's a basic technique:

Dissolve and resolve fear by first grounding in the ULF. Do this by remembering your true enlightened nature self, what the Buddhists call the "View," the ultimately positive and safe character of the ULF.

Breathe Love and Light into the sensation of fear and reassure yourself with the knowledge that everything is okay, it is only a feeling. Grounding to the positive first is important. If you try to clear fear from fear, the position the ego operates from, the chances of the fear being healed is much less.

Ground in your Being first. Remember the Love. Visualize and breathe love and light into the fear. Keep breathing. Reassure any fearful messages that emanate from the fear. For example, when the fear says, "No, don't go there, you're going to die," respond with "It may feel like I'm going to die, but I'm not." Or "Yes, someday my body will die, but I am eternal spirit and will live beyond the physical" or "It's good for me to feel this and I will feel better when it is released." While you don't have to say all of that every time, that's the message and, most importantly, the truth. Even the ego has a hard time arguing with the truth.

Releasing yourself from stored fearful emotional content releases you from having these unpleasant feelings constantly affecting your mood and life. The downside is temporarily feeling fearful vs. the upside of feeling better overall and attracting better things into your life.

According to *A Course in Miracles,* (see Recommended Books) there are only two emotions—love and fear. All the others are derivations of these two basic feeling energies. All the unpleasant, so called "negative" emotions like sadness and hurt, are fear-based and in the province of the ego. I have used fear as the example because for most people it is the most difficult to feel and let go. This process can be used for all other feelings including sadness and hurt. Sadness and hurt are most often simply and effectively released by crying.

The ego will always try to preserve its dominant role by throwing fear-based emotions at you to distract you from realizing your true nature. In fact, the more you evolve and spend time in your being, the more your ego becomes afraid and tries even harder to pull you back into fearful thinking. Its messages of fear are all untrue.

Remember, ultimately there is nothing to fear. Everything is peace, unity and compassion, not fear and division. If you are experiencing fear, or fear-based emotions, it means you've become lost in egoland and need to return home. Choose the love-based reality and embrace your experience of yourself and your feelings with compassion.

Appendix B – Changing Beliefs Process

IF YOU LEARN how to change your limiting core beliefs, you will have the power to significantly change your life for the better.

Techniques vary and are basically simple. The structure common to most approaches is to allow the existing limiting belief to surface, formulate the antithetical and truthful present day affirmation, and repeat it. The following exercise will work for all types of beliefs. It does require a bit of effort and you may have to push through some of your own resistance. Since beliefs regarding self-esteem and self-worth are probably the most important, we'll use them as an example.

1. **Discover and examine beliefs that are barriers to loving yourself.**

   Begin by brainstorming and writing down multiple answers to questions like:

   I am not okay because _____ .

   I am not worthy because _____ .

   I am no good because _____ .

   I am not deserving because _____ .

   I am not worth loving because _____ .

I am bad because _____ .

Example : I'm not okay because:

I'm too fat.

I'm not smart enough.

I'm irresponsible.

I'm unhappy.

You should add any personal negative labels you think about yourself, like I'm a loser, or I'm a jerk because _____ .

Brainstorm your answers for each question with as many responses that come to mind. Write them all down. Do this three or four times over a span of a couple of weeks. The more you do it the more the beliefs will surface. As you go through your day they will pop up in your head. Whenever they do, write them down.

2. Consolidate the lists.

Gather all your lists and the scraps of paper you jotted notes on. Some beliefs will show up repeatedly. These are your "core beliefs." By the end of two weeks you will have a sense of which ones are your biggest barriers. Core beliefs are the deeper, earlier, more ingrained beliefs. These will stand out and seem more true, like "that's not a belief, that a fact."

3. Start with a couple of your most prominent beliefs.

Consider that they are simply beliefs about your reality and not necessarily what is true. Know that all self-depreciating beliefs are lies you have believed to be true. Know that the truth is that you (as all people) are naturally okay and good at your core.

4. Write the opposite true statement for each belief.

Examples:

Belief	→	Opposite/Truth
I'm not okay because I'm insecure.		I'm insecure at times and I'm okay.
I'm not deserving because I'm bad.		I'm deserving because I'm good.
I'm not okay because I'm fat.		I'm overweight and I'm okay.
I'm bad because I've caused people pain.		I have caused hurt and I'm okay.
I can't love myself because it is a sin.		Loving myself is not a sin.
I'm not okay because I'm not attractive.		I'm worthy of my love, regardless of appearance.

None of your negative beliefs or judgments affect your true self. Your ULF core is naturally okay and worthy. Remind yourself that your self worth is not dependant on whether or not you have a boyfriend, girlfriend, husband, wife, money, job, car, arms, legs, or anything. You are naturally okay and a worthwhile being. You may not believe this at first. That's okay too. But do these exercises even if you do not yet believe in your new statement.

Adjust the wording of your new beliefs until they directly confront your old belief and feel correct. Make your statements as short as possible. Enlist the help of a skilled friend or therapist if you have difficulty developing the truthful counterparts to your depreciating beliefs. Examine and repeat the new statements. Know that they are true.

You will not believe them at first. Ask yourself, would you believe these same beliefs to be true about other people? Do you think that a person's self worth is really dependant on appearance? If you don't believe that it's true for others why would you think it's true about you? Some things may seem undeniably "bad." Remember, a child may do something "bad" but that does not make the child inherently bad as a person. The same truth applies to you.

5. **Relax and repeat these statements for 5-10 minutes, twice a day for 30 days. Feel them as deeply as you can.**

Experience any emotional reactions or thoughts that arise when repeating the new statements. In the beginning, the part of you that doesn't believe your new truths will protest. It will seem like the old belief is true and the new belief is false. Stick with it; after a while the new belief will start to replace the old one. New beliefs can be audio recorded and played back so that all you have to do is relax and listen. This can make things easier and more likely you will stay with the program.

Initially, it is useful to bring up and confront these core beliefs with any phrasing that is accurate for you. For example, if your belief is "I'm not OK because I'm fat," it would be useful to directly counter that false belief with a truthful statement like, "My Okayness, or self worth, has nothing to do with how much I weigh." Your conscious brain begins to confront and acknowledge that what you believe and what is actually true, are different. You start to realize and believe that, "Gee, my Okayness really isn't dependent on how much I weigh!" Any statement that expresses the truth will help dislodge old beliefs and adopt new, truer ones.

Eventually it becomes important to pay attention to an interesting fact. It turns out the subconscious doesn't understand any words of negation, like "not" or "no" or "nothing," and will drop these out of any new core belief you are creating. This is especially important for any deep meditative or sleep programming you might do with your new beliefs. As you begin to deeply affirm your new beliefs or play a recording of your beliefs using a timer to program your unconscious mind while sleeping, you must avoid negatives like "I'm not" and "no."

For example, if my new truthful belief is "Loving myself is not a sin," the subconscious doesn't understand the "not" part and it drops it out. It hears, "Loving myself is a sin". That is not what is true or what you want to affirm. As you begin to consciously reject the old beliefs and become more comfortable with the truthfulness of your new beliefs it, is best to refine them into completely positive affirmations. Leave out the negatives and go with something like, "Loving myself is good," or "It's okay to love myself." Getting these phrases right for you may be a little tricky but it becomes easier as you spend more time with them.

You may want to ask a good friend for their support, someone who won't let you off the hook. Make a commitment to yourself, and your friend, to help motivate yourself. Give yourself some reward for keeping your commitment and make sure it's big enough to motivate you.

6. Repeat as needed.

Most people find that after doing the process, a negative core belief stands out or new ones emerge. Simply repeat the process. You will know when you have been successful when the new belief feels true. Often only one or two cycles are needed to reap noticeable benefits.

Recommended Books

Highly Recommended Non-Fiction

This is not a bibliography of all the books synthesized in this "field guide." Rather, it is a list of books that I believe can have the most impact on readers.

Tibetan Book of the Living and Dying by Sogyal Rinpoche.
There are many hard-to-understand translations/explanations of the Tibetan Book of the Dead, which describes what happens during the transition between lifetimes and how to prepare for it. This is by far the best, most accessible and enlightening, plus the first half of the book could be called "Secrets of Buddhism Revealed."

A Course in Miracles published by Foundation for Inner Peace.
Sold separately, or as a combined volume, it consists of a trilogy of three books: a *Text*, a *Workbook for Students* comprised of 365 lessons or meditations for each day of a year, and a *Manual for Teachers*, which is often recommended to be read first. Purportedly written by the Christ Consciousness and channeled through an originally unwilling participant, Dr. Helen Schucman, a Jewish psychologist who lived from 1909-1981. As wild as it sounds, when you read the writings, the information is of such mind altering depth that it seems implausible to have come from Dr. Schucman writing on her own.

(While some discredit channeling, weren't the writers of the books of the Bible supposedly channeling the word of God?) It updates Christianity, becoming in essence a new, New Testament. The language is intellectually challenging and somewhat difficult to understand, (made more so by the fact that the ego doesn't want to hear it), but contains some of the most profound writings available to date.

A Talk Given on a Course of Miracles by Kenneth Wapnick, PhD.
A short, easy to understand explanation of *A Course in Miracles.*

Awaken from the Dream: A Presentation of a Course in Miracles by Kenneth Wapnick, PhD.
If you've got a bit more time, this is a more in-depth explanation that is profound yet easy to read.

Power of Now by Eckhart Tolle.
Explains better than anyone else the difference between the two states of reality: thinking vs. the being in now and why it makes sense to be in the present.

Recommended Non-Fiction

Auto-Biography of a Yogi by Paramahansa Yogananda.
There's something about this book; even his picture on the cover seems to communicate to you directly. He says and describes things that couldn't rationally happen, yet his words ring of truth. A bona fide guru's story of the evolution and life of a true spiritual master.

Scientific Healing Affirmations by Paramahansa Yogananda.
A miniature book on healing; one of the best, with a fascinating, matter-of-fact explanation of the "Nature of Creation."

Everyday Miracles, the Inner Art of Manifestation by David Spangler.
A spiritual philosopher, teacher, writer, and former co-director of Findhorn, a New Age community in northern Scotland. If I was to recommend one book on manifestation this is it.

Who Dies by Steven Levine.
Like many, I avoided reading about death even after the death of a significant other. I wish I had read it earlier. Tremendously helpful for those dealing death and dying. Levine, a Buddhist, teacher, and former student of Elizabeth Kubler-Ross, speaks clearly and profoundly on these matters. He has written many excellent books and this is a great one to start with.

Seth Books by Jane Roberts.
Roberts began as many "channels" have, doing automatic writing. She soon felt compelled to speak responses to questions and began channeling for a disembodied entity who called himself Seth. Fearing she was losing her mind, she sought professional help and was assured she was not schizophrenic. The information is so deep and of a different voice that is seems unlikely that the material comes from her. Profound and clear with a reality-changing view.

- 1st book – *The Seth Material* describes how Ms. Roberts began channeling for Seth; the meat of the material is in the 2nd and 3rd books.

- 2nd book – *Seth Speaks: The Eternal Validity of the Soul* deals with the structure of reality.

- 3rd book – *Seth Speaks: The Nature of Personal Reality* speaks more of the individual's journey and meta-psychology. (See the website for a book report/summary of this book.)

Touching Peace by Thich Nhat Hanh.
Buddhist monk, author, scholar, and poet; short, sweet, and deep experience of peace.

Guilt is the Teacher, Love is the Lesson by Joan Borysenko.
Don't let the title put you off; it's the best explanation and synthesis of science and psycho-spirituality I've come across. If you had to give one book to a person interested in this topic, this is the book.

Love, Medicine and Miracles by Bernie Siegel.
The title says it well. A cancer surgeon who was brave enough to stand up and say, "Hey, look at this, this is really important!" He freely admits he didn't start mind/body medicine, but he was the guy that brought it to our modern culture. Great review of the ground-breaking intersection of medical science, psychology and spirituality. Healing and inspirational.

Quantum Healing: Exploring the Frontiers of Mind/Body Medicine by Deepak Chopra.
His first book, excellent , well written, best summary of mind/body medicine.

Mind, Fantasy and Healing by Alice Hopper-Epstein.
She successfully used psycho-synthesis therapy to heal herself of a terminal cancer. Psycho-synthesis is a psycho-therapy developed by Italian psychiatrist Robert Assignoli in which the therapist brings you on a trance healing journey through your inner self, accompanied by your imagination of wise, internal guidance to meet and greet your sub-personalities and discover and release events, beliefs and fears they may be holding onto and no longer need to. A very powerful, enjoyable and effective therapy!

Life After Life: The Investigation of a Phenomenon: Survival of Bodily Death by Raymond Moody.
Research and accounts of what the first steps into the afterlife look like. This is the book that started it all regarding Near Death Experiences. Well researched and written.

Fairies at Work and Play by Geoffrey Hodson.
Written in the 1920's in England by a gentleman able to see all sorts of "little people" and verified in the preface by another gentleman who also can "see" into this dimension. Written in such a matter-of-fact reporting style you get the sense that this person is seeing into another reality. It opens up a whole new world!

Human Operator's Manual: How Feelings Work, A Psychological Primer by Stuart Zelman, Ph.D., and David Bognar.
This book is a psychological primer, a manual on understanding feelings and how people function internally and emotionally. The book explains exactly what feelings are, how they work, how we avoid

them, and what happens to avoided feelings. It explains how these old feelings color our experience and perceptions, create pain, disease, and block positive experience. The book explains how to regain full access to experience, and the benefits and process of releasing old feelings. Information on self-help basics makes up the final section, including communicating emotions, the change process, self esteem, attitude, and information on choosing a therapist.

Pathwork of Self Transformation by Eva Pierrakos.
John Pierrakos was a psychiatrist and cofounder of Bioenergetics along with the better known Alexander Lowen. Pierrakos married Eva who turned out to be a trance channel providing succinct, powerful, in-depth information on how to undo emotional and energetic blocks. This is some of the most powerful information on the psychological process of attaining spiritual self-realization and unification with God Essence/Core. Like the *Course in Miracles,* the truth often creates an incredible amount of ego resistance: resistance so fierce that it is often hard to read. Free transcripts of channeled lectures given on a very interesting range of topics are available on an international foundation web site. (See "Links" at www.EnlightenmentMadeSimple.com.)

Secret Life of Plants by Peter Tompkins and Christopher Bird.
I never finished this book, because I was so blown away by what I read in the first 100 pages. Plants able to sense emotions, researchers developing bio sensors, plants proven to be able to transmit and receive through solid matter – wow stuff.

The Field: The Quest for the Secret Force of the Universe by Lynne McTaggart.

A journalist summarizes the latest research into quantum physics. There really is a new vs. old science change going on in the world. In the old science, everything was a particle with defined edges, but the new science has basically proven that everything is a wave and possibly a particle. Another one of those books that blew me away in the first 100 pages. World and reality altering discoveries. The opening summary of what is happening in the world of science is worth the price of the book. Astonishing. Well done.

Triangles from the Lucis Trust.

A series of free booklets and pamphlets about a meditative concept that serves humanity. Originates in a series of books written by Alice Bailey in collaboration with an eastern spiritual master called "the Tibetan." Individuals mentally join in groups of threes to visualize a triangular grid of healing energy around the earth that focuses energy of good will to humanity and the planet. Fascinating material and a productive avenue for those wishing to contribute to the greater good. (See "Links" at www.EnlightenmentMadeSimple.com.)

Recommended Fiction

The Education of Oversoul Seven by Jane Roberts.

A fictional account based on the Seth information regarding the structure of our reality. A story of a non-physical entity named Oversoul 7 who has three distinct physical sub-personalities on earth at three different time periods, and a "higher self" who helps him along.

Illusions: The Adventures of a Reluctant Messiah by Richard Bach.
A fun, educational and inspiring easy read.

What Dreams May Come by Richard Matheson.
You may have seen the movie with Robin Williams that was based on this novel. Matheson, introduces this "fictional" work by asserting that the only thing that is fictional about it are the characters because it is based on his extensive research regarding the after-death experience. He has a very lengthy and interesting bibliography in the back of the book. Besides being a fascinating depiction of life in the non-physical dimension, the book helps open the mind and spirit of the reader to the existence of this realm and spirit helpers.

Photography by David Bognar

Photography by David Bognar

Photo Editing – Pat Minicucci
Tag Clouds generated by Wordle

About the Author

David Bognar's quest for answers began with reading a book about Raja Yoga and practicing meditation at age 15. Pursuing his intense curiosity about people, psychology, and the metaphysical he became a voracious reader and explored countless therapies, spiritual disciplines and techniques. While working as a mental health worker and treatment coordinator he deepened his understanding of psychology by participating in numerous workshops and trainings. He discovered that accurate and understandable information about feelings essential for emotional well being was hard to find. In 1991, he wrote the book, *The Human Operators Manual – How Feelings Work: a Psychological Primer*, with Dr. Stewart Zelman.

Wanting to see helpful psychological information be more readily available he decided television was an ideal medium. To learn the craft, he worked as a cable television studio manager, as well as at a "new age" film production company. He developed ideas and scripts, and produced and edited local television shows and documentaries. After cancer claimed the life of his girlfriend at the untimely age of thirty-three, David painstakingly researched, wrote and produced *CANCER: Increasing Your Odds for Survival* – a comprehensive overview of information and resources to assist cancer patients in surviving cancer. Walter Cronkite narrated the award winning four-hour public television series, which aired nationally and focused on mind/body medicine and the psychological and spiritual components of healing.

David also researched and wrote the highly praised companion book, *CANCER: Increasing Your Odds for Survival, A Resource Guide for the Integrating Mainstream, Alternative, and Complementary Therapies,* published by Hunter House.

After 40 years of research into the "big questions" of life, David wrote *Enlightenment,* a psycho-spiritual primer. He is motivated by the fact that information about psychology and spirituality can help people suffer less and enjoy life more. By presenting this information, in a concise and easy-to-understand manner, he hopes that greater numbers of people will benefit from this knowledge.

LaVergne, TN USA
30 April 2010
180999LV00002B